To Michelle - my Blue Angel.

-Robert

The LUCKY Blue Angel

Robert Flynn

illustrated by
Kevin Coffey

Lucky McGuire loves to fly! Every day he and his friends launch from their home on the aircraft carrier and into the sky.

Today is a special day for Lucky. It is his last flight on the aircraft carrier until he moves away. Navy jets move to places where they are needed and travel the world. After he lands, his friends are giving him a going away party!

The sky was bright blue and the sun was warm but suddenly Lucky felt sad. He didn't want to leave his friends. He wanted to stay and fly with them every day. Also, Lucky didn't know where the Navy was sending him next. He had dreamed of being a Blue Angel but it didn't look like that was going to happen. He hoped that wherever he was sent, he would make friends and get to fly.

But it wasn't time to land
and Lucky wanted to make the
most of the clear and sunny day. He
rocketed into the sky doing loops and rolls
and flying upside down. He wished it could last
forever! But it was time to get back to the aircraft
carrier and Navy jets are never late.

Lucky pointed his nose toward home and turned on his afterburner jets! He streaked across the sky going faster than the speed of sound! He wanted to make his best landing ever.

Landing on an aircraft carrier was not easy. But Lucky was one of the greatest. He loved the challenge! He flew the best that he could until he landed with a thunderous BANG! A perfect landing! All the aircraft on the flight deck cheered for Lucky.

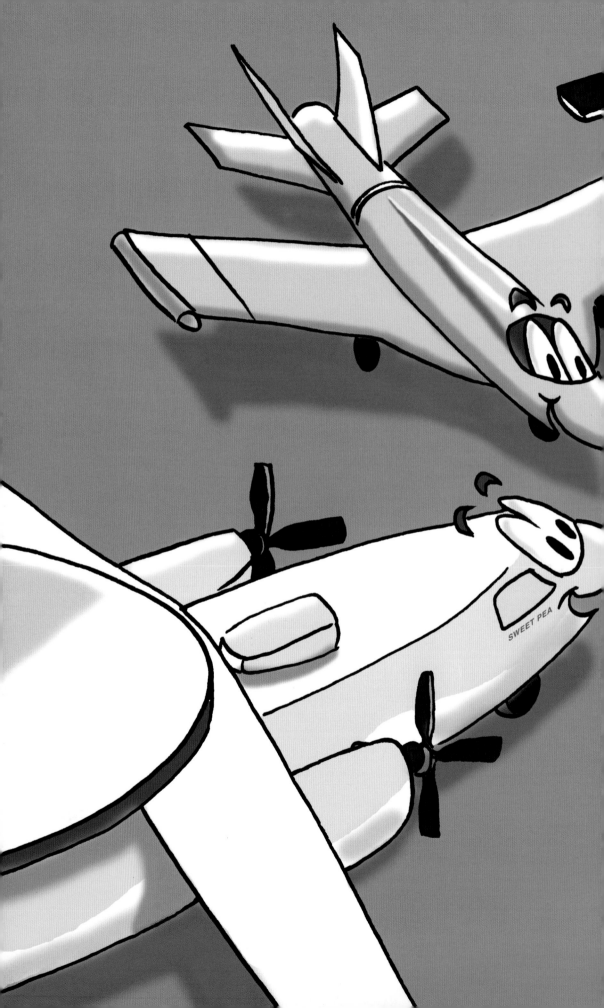

"Good luck at the maintenance depot, Lucky," said his friend Pepper. "Do you know where they are sending you after you are finished with your check-up at the maintenance depot?" asked Swerve. "They haven't told me yet," replied Lucky worriedly.

"Did you ever hear if you made the Blue Angels, Lucky?" asked Sweet Pea. "They take the best Navy and Marine Corps jets. I know you always dreamed of being a Blue Angel!" "No," said Lucky. "The Blue Angels didn't call me. I guess I didn't make the team."

"Just stay away from the aircraft storage yard in the desert," joked Millhouse, "they cover you in plastic and all you do is sit in the hot sun all day long. Nobody flies away from the desert!"

The next day Lucky launched from his home on the aircraft carrier for the last time. He was sad as he waved goodbye to his buddies.

The maintenance depot was a place where they fixed airplanes and made sure that they were healthy and strong. The mechanics and engineers were like doctors to an airplane.

They took very good care of Lucky. They put new oil in his engines and new rivets in his wings. They were even going to give him a new coat of paint.

Lucky wondered where he would be sent next. Even if he couldn't be a Blue Angel, he just hoped that he could fly every day. Maybe he would be sent to Test Pilot School where he could do spins and fly high and fast?

Or maybe they would send him to train young airplanes how to fly off of aircraft carriers?

But what if they covered him in plastic and sent him to the hot, dry desert to be put in the storage yard and never let him fly? Lucky was worried. He missed his friends. He wanted to fly again.

The next day it was time for Lucky's last coat of paint. After the paint dried, the maintenance Chief told Lucky it was time to go.

"Where am I going?" asked Lucky nervously.

"They are waiting for you in the desert," the Chief replied. But Lucky didn't want to go to the desert. He wanted to fly!

"Chief, there must be a mistake. They can't be sending me to the desert," Lucky pleaded. "I feel great! I am flying better than ever. Please, Chief, don't send me to the desert!"

"That is what your orders say, McGuire," replied the Chief. "You know better than anybody, Lucky. We do what we are told in the U.S. Navy."

Lucky was disappointed. He didn't want to go, but Navy jets follow orders. Lucky rolled slowly out of the hangar. He caught a glimpse of his reflection in the hangar door. He didn't look like himself. When he arrived, he was gray like most of the other aircraft in the Navy.

But now his paint was shiny and glistened in the sun. He was brilliant blue with gold stripes . . . those were the colors of the Blue Angels!

"Hey, Lucky!" shouted one of the maintenance chiefs. "You better get your afterburners in gear! Your team is waiting for you in the desert!"

Could it be true? Lucky couldn't believe it! Lucky McGuire was going to be a Blue Angel! Lucky was so excited he flew supersonic speed all the way there. The team was practicing in the desert before they went home to beautiful Pensacola, Florida for their show season!

Lucky made great friends on his new team. The Blue Angels performed for millions of people, spreading goodwill and representing the U.S. Navy and Marine Corps. And best of all, they got to fly together every day!

About the author

CDR Bob "Flynner" Flynn is a career Naval Flight Officer
who has served tours on multiple aircraft carriers as well as
various staff and overseas assignments. His wife Michelle
is a Commander in the Navy Reserve and former Blue Angel
Supply Officer. They met in Pensacola, Florida, and now
live with their three children in Rhode Island.